Bumble
A Haiku Collection
by Ashley Centers

---

bum·ble: 1. move or act in an awkward or confused manner; 2. speak in a confused or indistinct way

---

Copyright

Collection © 2018 by Ashley Centers; individual haikus published in past years on social media. All rights reserved; no part of this book may be reproduced in whole or in part in any form without express written permission from the author.

Acknowledgements

This book has very deep, very personal roots in my own life. There are several people and relationships embedded within this book, and while names are not provided, these experiences and relationships are perhaps the most important aspects of my life. While these poems are both painful and joyous in nature, it has never been my intention to cause any pain. I just need to say thank you for everything and that I love you.

This book would have not been possible without many people.
First, I'd like to thank Sylvia Gray for challenging me to write something short in form and to keep doing it, and to Christine Locker for jumping on board with my crazy ideas and disorganized thoughts. Thank you for making my biggest dream come true. I'll be forever grateful. The talented Lauren Paterson with *Muse Media Co.* has designed the beautiful cover art. Jonathan Gradin provided typesetting magic. And to so many others: My Mama, Brother, T, Kelsey, Heather, Dustin, Wendy, and countless others for constantly lifting me up when I'm down, pushing me when I feel like I can't go an inch further, and calling me on my nonsense when needed.

Finally, this is for *you*.
You, who feel lost and alone.
You are brave. *You* are strong.
You are capable. *You* are worthy.
You are so incredibly loved.

Can you keep secrets?
Lines cross. Love sways. We teeter.
Shields drop down hard.

Rain splashes concrete.
Their hearts beat contentedly.
Please, stay awhile?

Stream of baby puke.
Ah, bright eyes, full of wonder.
Leave the rest alone.

Nightmares awake me.
Meditate my fears away.
Will I sleep tonight?

Everybody asks
what my future will look like.
I have no answer.

Sweltering summer,
full bellies and content hearts.
Remember these days.

Up and down and 'round—
feelings all over the place.
Attachment is hard.

The touch of your hand—
we are made to be broken.
Breathe in and let go.

Gratitude is love:
Learning to let others help.
Control is not mine.

Wherever you are,
love will shine down upon you.
Don't be so fearful.

Conflicting feelings,
unsure how to express them.
You won't understand.

I am here to stay.
Words heavy with their meaning.
Be content, my heart.

Shoes. Makeup. Fauxhawk.
Drag show cherry pops tonight.
My life be like woah.

I've been here before:
This clean house with candles lit
reminds me of home.

Why is it that we
mourn the famous but treat our
neighbors with cruelty?

When you realize
you cannot be in control,
it will all work out.

Open your heart up
to love in her purest form—
anticipation.

Always wanting more
love instead friends, coffee, books.
These are what matter.

She takes to flight when
the days become insipid
and the nights lonely.

Your love makes me weak.
There you go breaking my heart.
The weight of silence.

And words escape her.
Left alone with her nightmares:
The end is coming.

Back and forth. Back. Forth.
She will always win your heart.
Just friends, remember?

Maybe I should stop
this love. Get my head on straight…
It's not that easy.

Sorry for showing
all sorts of crazyface feels.
Times are uncertain.

This is what you get—
feel the fear slipping back in.
Sleep, drink, and repeat.

Mega explosions
of growth and constant motion,
and still, thoughts of you.

Reminder to self:
We are all works in progress;
forgiveness goes far.

No more school for me.
Fool enough for no degree.
I will have purpose.

Worry yourself sick
or surrender and feel peace.
Don't be so stubborn.

Grow, change, live, and feel.
Like poison-infused honey—
sweet tinged with bitter.

Vibrations travel
through paper walls. I wonder
if I'm missing out.

Something is awry.
Strange dreams, quiet, heaviness.
Life has been curtailed.

Hello there, sunshine.
He proffers a hug, cheeks flush.
Some nights will live on.

And I sleep to dream.
When my thoughts turn to your love…
How to be alone?

So many people—
expectations you won't meet.
Remember to breathe.

Play some hide and seek
and light my cold heart on fire.
Pain is cathartic.

One broken wheelchair,
got a black eye playing pool.
My friends are the best.

Moody and mellow—
drowning in sad yesterdays.
Can you forgive me?

Ebb, flow, and the rush
of the years passing me by.
Time to fly or fall.

Disappointment in
my stagnant nature. Movement
is the hardest fight.

Can't hide my hot mess—
sinus headache, spilled coffee…
Saving grace in friends.

Birds chirp morning songs.
Pumpkin chai. Baby snuggles.
Little things bring joy.

Follow the moonlight.
Fly away to somewhere new.
Fool these winter blues.

I hear your voice and
all my troubles disappear.
Nothing else matters.

Will this black balloon
carry me off? Please say this
isn't all there is.

Don't say a word, dear.
Pretend for just a minute
that you still loved me.

Do not get attached.
Even stars collapse into
voids of nothingness.

Your fears will drown you.
Stuck in reverse and afraid.
Follow the light home.

Poems are hard when
friends demand hyperboles
and happiness, too.

Oh, I love people,
but solitude means quiet
for this anxious mind.

Broken wheels don't hurt
so much when surrounded by
friends, sun and music.

Weary hearts quiet,
knowing the body is a
temporary home.

I imagine you,
ball of incessant motion,
storming the heavens.

Dreams of a naïve
girl who didn't know better
make for harsh lessons.

Escape confinement,
stand, stretch your tired body.
Free your mind's monsters.

She finds her daydreams
and biggest fears occupy
the same space within.

What do life or death
matter when surrounded by
light? Fear consumes her.

Connection runs deep
in secret smiles and blue eyes
haunted by the past.

I wait for you still,
even though you aren't coming.
I should know better.

She looks for something
to ease the pain. Don't forget
real peace lies within.

Why today is good:
Bright clothing, too much coffee,
the laughter of friends.

You've made your choice clear.
She is your greatest love. And
my love grows quiet.

I disappoint you
when I fail to find a job,
but I'm so afraid.

Let me change your world,
and maybe you'll see the stars
align in our eyes.

They wander around
in the dark so they don't have
to go home alone.

She's teetering on
the edge again. Her blue mind
will swallow her whole.

I can't seem to fill
the empty spot in my heart
where you wrote your name.

These words on my skin,
pretend none of it matters.
Broken hearts beat on.

Hurricanes crash down,
and the orange sky whispers,
"Where is your God now?"

Contentment arrives
at two in the morning when
you say, "Hello, love."

Don't let knowledge that
you'll spend your life alone make
for a bitter heart.

Because government
has no place in a marriage,
Love prevails today.

Today might be dark
because grief is more than death.
But you are enough.

She's taken to flight
as to avoid the mirrors
in her glass castle.

Loving this body
means a cute dress and fauxhawk
on the worst of days.

Rockabye, baby.
I hope you can feel the love
this world holds for you.

Love means boundaries.
Brown eyes, remember that you
are the only one.

You walk out the door
as I promise this broken
heart is not your fault.

When the booze wears off
and the band lays down their souls,
I'm still here: empty.

Numbers, love and God:
Things that keep me from sleep when
the world grows quiet.

Because seven years
makes for a damn heavy weight,
You're slipping away.

She wakes overwhelmed
and scared but is quick to feel
the love that surrounds.

Pathetic. Lazy.
Fat. These words will not break me.
You can't understand.

She's coming down from
the ledge she's been living on.
Watch your step, darling.

When there's nothing left
to say and you need a break
from the world, just breathe.

Remember these tears
because good will come from them.
Rest easy now, child.

Month of gratitude,
but really, I'm blessed each day
with the best people.

Don't forget small things
mean the most: hot cider, friends,
and vitamin D.

To change Idaho
for the better, we must vote
our governor out.

Her biggest fault is
that she cares too much about
love. Learn to say no.

Poetry is me
in the raw. Vulnerable.
Pouring out my soul.

You see the wheelchair
and fat but seem to forget
the she underneath.

Feel this rebel heart
beat as she dreams of Never
Neverland and light.

Alone in the dark
with the monsters in my head.
Can't make you love me.

Cast your fears into
the perfect wilderness of
your fledgling pink heart.

I won't cry this time
as you walk away. Play me
a redemption song.

Tomorrow exists
in all the hearts we can't see
living with closed minds.

Watch as she meets sweet
dreams and know that everything
ends just as it should.

Rain pours from gray skies,
and there's a girl in the war,
screaming from rooftops.

She asks, desperate,
"Show me something beautiful."
He says to let go.

We don't need words. Take
me somewhere only we know.
And forget the rest.

Justice won't be served
while racism thrives. Guilty white
cops on power trips.

I find an old friend
has come to play. Oh Lord, please
go easy on me.

On midnight walks home,
laughter fills the empty street.
Cigarette glows bright.

The poor boy has lost
his head looking for release.
Watch his spirit fade.

Escape from my head
because thoughts of you leave me
drowning in the dark.

Stand by me, darling—
room full of pretty faces,
connection runs deep.

Break down at his touch,
and promise you'll sleep tonight.
"Iris" on repeat.

Left craving the taste
of his skin, but she'd settle
for a dreamless sleep.

A world gone shallow
leaves little room for quiet
in this weary heart.

Words spill out, release.
"Relax," he says. But the drugs
don't work anymore.

Truth leaves you open,
vulnerable. Others see
only what they want.

After all these years,
you see right through me. Sometimes,
love means letting go.

A long December.
Watch as she burns in these flames
she struck, bright and hot.

And on the last day,
she found happiness starts with
the spark of a flame.

Let the darkest day
be filled with light and laughter
of crazy Russians.

This can't mean to you
what it means to me. Look back
as I catch myself.

Words pour out red lips,
and music bleeds from my veins.
I cannot find you.

Two lost souls wander
empty streets: Bursts of laughter,
beer, quiet sorrow.

Quiet can be found
In fresh snowfall, hot cocoa,
books, and a ballad.

Even the brightest
stars get caught in the shadow
of the moon's surface.

She holds her breath tight,
waiting for him to come 'round
and bleed her heart dry.

So much left unsaid—
now my feet won't touch the ground.
You should still be here.

He'll come around when
life breaks him down, and she prays,
dear God, for the strength.

The world falls silent,
plummeting away, embraced
by dreams of music.

I still think of you
on winter mornings as fog
swallows the sky whole.

Heaviness erupts,
and he grieves complete freedom;
stuck in love and war.

Halfway to sunrise,
and she's made friends with the ghost
of memory past.

Seven years later,
and you make walking away
look so damn easy.

Blue mind, broken wheel,
and still missing you. Tell me,
how do we fix this?

Turn on the bright lights,
and break down the walls you've built.
Let love surround you.

She fills her days with
people, her nights with music.
Praying for life's end.

Look how the stars shine
when you feel alone. Love is
more than a feeling.

Watch her heart turn cold
to match this empty bed. Run
as far as you can.

Grief is more than death.
It's an empty heart struggling
to fill itself up.

Quick, pick yourself up.
Falling apart is ugly
and most burdensome.

Day breaks; she finds she's
not meeting expectations.
Some things never change.

Things I'll never say:
I miss you terribly. I
want you in my life.

And at the day's end,
fill yourself with light because
you're worthy of love.

And eight weeks later,
she sees better days ahead.
Here is to goodbye.

She wakes up to find
her world spinning, and she's lost
Somewhere in the dark.

When the right words fail,
just listen to your heart's yearn.
I can't walk away.

Gloomy skies threaten
to plunge her back in darkness,
where monsters roam free.

When life gets heavy
let your blue mind find solace
in a bigger love.

Good days are made of
friends, both new and old, coffee,
music, bright sunsets.

And just so you know,
she wants to fly; disappear
deep in the night sky.

Broken vows arrive
in Sunday morning phone calls
and your guilty voice.

Things to remember:
You are capable, enough,
and free. Tread softly.

And she cannot find
even ground to catch her breath—
spinning in circles.

Brown eyes, will you help
me forget all the ways in
which you loved me well?

Because you loved me
much too well, this blue mind is
leading me to hell.

Lay these weary bones
down, and surrender your pain.
Shadows dance in blue.

Drifting toward sleep,
she asks for one more song, please?
"Be here now," he says.

Spend a weekend in
Neverland, where time stands still,
and your dreams come true.

Ah! Nostalgia is
a warm summer day with you.
Fate had her own plans.

Let your heart hold fast
to this moment when old loves
yesterday threaten.

Wake up overwhelmed
at dreams from another life.
Wish upon a star.

Confessions of a
young woman, sad and selfish,
but always learning.

The world lays quiet
and her bed empty because
she cannot forget.

When you cannot sleep
and old heartaches swell inside,
turn the lights out, love.

You ask who it is
that I've been missing. Brown eyes,
it's always been you.

Hot water sprays, scalds
her pink skin, warm to the touch.
Burn these desires down.

Early morn' phone calls
and things I'll never say, but
you already know.

Shhh, don't make a scene.
Maybe they've forgotten how
exhausting you are.

This means naught to you
what it means to me. Rebounds
are not meant for love.

Electric blue nails
and plum colored hair. Life is
more than black and white.

She gives everything
to feel numb. Don't forget to
come up for air, love.

Six days before you
leave on a jet plane. Some aches
throb incessantly.

I want you to know
life is a strange condition.
Keep moving forward.

Please don't be afraid
to sink into the blue. Watch
you drifting on by.

You're going to be
a dad (again). Maybe now
we can move forward.

She's craving some light
and a quick way out. Blue is
the deepest color.

You can't find the words
to release the pain inside.
Turn the volume up.

Watch your face light up
as his shadow nears, pipe smoke
trailing his moon dance.

His voice tempts, but you
cannot stay the night. It hurts
too damn much this time.

You and your guitar
in my dark living room, and
I can't stop the tears.

Watch your fiery dance,
and aches I thought were buried
swell up. I can't breathe.

All I really want
is to feel the fire raging
with a love like yours.

And empathy is
intensely feeling your pain
'cross the ocean blue.

And I lose my words
with you. One look inside your
big browns, and I'm gone.

Can you free yourself
enough to absolve the hurt
and open your heart?

She's gone away now,
and he prays it's not the last
time he's seen her light.

Living in the stars,
and you steal my breath away.
Catch these salty tears.

Wake up and pretend
you aren't breaking to pieces.
And this too shall pass.

Release me from sin,
and I'll practice redemption;
more heart, less attack.

Memory: Falling
asleep on the phone with your
voice as my cocoon.

Lips of cheap, red wine,
but you hold the universe
in those sad eyes, boy.

Are you happy now
with this life built on lies and
broken promises?

Sitting in the dark
and you grab my hand. Watch these
blues shine bright tonight.

Dizzy up the girl;
ride this merry-go-round of
love as she crumbles.

Small things rushing back:
A midnight drive, first kisses
from a sweet baby.

Close those sleepy eyes,
and let the fire consume you;
burn these desires down.

Emptiness stalks her
into the night, where she longs
for a dreamless sleep.

Let go of your fear,
and understand everything
ends just as it should.

Words kaleidoscope
inside my head, and the world
whirls subtly 'round me.

Watch these crushing waves
of sadness come before you,
and so you just breathe.

Overdose on your
love just to find it nothing
more than a child's game.

Won't you remember
that not life nor love exist
in God's black and white?

So I'm unsteady,
overwhelmed by memory
and life without you.

And so he breaks her
heart wide open with music:
I love you. Goodbye.

Twenty-one goodbyes,
and grey skies so I can feel
you near one last time.

Love will break us down;
meanwhile, desperation binds,
and everyone hurts.

Life seems nothing more
than hello and goodbye, but
I need you to stay.

Paris is burning,
and our green earth is melting.
Look what we have done.

Walk the empty streets
of Neverland. Can't you hear
echoes of laughter?

Let flickering lights
and crazy strong wind smother
these dark, lonely thoughts.

Overwhelmed again,
but she can't rush growth. Music,
friends keep her grounded.

Shadows become whole,
and sleep never was your thing.
Rise and meet the light.

Lay down your burdens,
and let this weary soul rest,
free of the mind's beasts.

How can you measure
fleeting years, save in sunsets,
distance, tears, and love?

Let love bring you home
when you can't find your way through
memories of him.

I'd cede forever
To touch you, feeling scars carved
from second chances.

When the night is long,
and your heart heavy with grief,
can you let it be?

Make a man of you—
pull the rope and watch the blood
drain from my blank face.

The stars turn to dust,
and love has torn us apart,
so you disappear.

And she fills you up
in ways that I never will,
hiding from the light.

Haunted by your ghost,
but it's time to get off this
love merry-go-round.

Oh, some lies settle
deep in hearts weary afraid
of changing their ways.

She doesn't know how
to let love go so she breaks
down and lets him in.

You deserve a chance
at the kind of love he can't
give you. Look inside.

Turn the music up,
and suddenly you know some
things can't be buried.

And they walk away
before his clothes are lying
on her bedroom floor.

Music notes drift and
memories flood from lyrics
of another life.

When the screaming stops,
and the fire burns away, you'll
see there's so much more.

Hollow enough to
know we're no good, but still miss
the light in your eyes.

Swallow these prayers
to a God you struggle with
to prove you worthy.

Love will be there on
your darkest, loneliest night.
This is not the end.

Shadows eat the moon,
and the night is yours alone
to survive within.

Your dreams await you
if only you'd stop spinning
long enough to try.

Raise up, bright eyes, 'cause
everybody needs you strong
when the lights go out.

Can't you see the man
you're made to be? Destined for
more than this small town.

Fake yellow lights to
drown out sleepless nights and the
memories of you.

Laughter bellows out
from cracked lips. Despite this, she
cannot find the light.

You are worthy of
more than empty promises
and pretty blue eyes.

Halfway to sunrise,
and you can't find your way out
of this fearful heart.

Can you believe in
the stars and a world made for
more than you and me?

She will wear him down
again, and they'll make small talk;
cages 'round their hearts.

And belief is hard
to swallow when you cannot
meet expectations.

Quickest way to break
a heart: "Nobody wants me."
You are so worthy.

Watch her curl inside
her broken spirit, looking
for a quick way out.

Watch her paint the blues
into this good feeling, 'cause
she cannot pretend.

Your babes are grown now,
and we're all stuck, wondering
why you had to leave.

Four in the morning,
and there she lay, head full of
fear, heart of sorrow.

She finds his aura
in a certain kind of light
she can't shake away.

Embrace arms full of
a babe heavy with sleep, and
the laughter of friends.

Draw you out of your
cocoon, and summon the Gods
to play us a song.

Her temple burns bright,
and the moon swallows the sun
as she is released.

Don't forget to breathe,
and know it's okay to cry;
we all make mistakes.

Tell me the things you've
been holding back from running
out those pretty lips.

Angry—you say I
cannot understand, but this
darkness feels like home.

Spiraling downward
into madness 'cause her fear
has swallowed the light.

Look your best so they
won't know you're making friends with
the monsters inside.

Front porch made of smoke;
hearts learning to trust after
oceans of heartache.

We skip rocks behind
the church and hope our demons
leave us to the light.

Wander these dark streets
until climbing into your
empty bed alone.

Close those weary eyes,
and let the music bring you
to the other side.

A song reminds you
forgiveness is a process
but you've been released.

Heads spinning again;
we'll play a game of hide and
seek with memory.

Dreams 'bout who we were
before love and grief and the
world fell at our feet.

Your love grows quiet,
and desperation leaves my
naïve heart exposed.

In a world full of
pretty faces, yours is the
one I can't forget.

Close those tired eyes,
and I'll sing a lullaby—
You are my sunshine.

Her cross grows heavy
with the sin of their bodies
tangled in the dark.

Some nights memory
is a bitter pill, swallowed
with prayers for sleep.

Words tumble out from
cider-stained lips with prayers
to a sometimes God.

Bones heavy with guilt
hold fast to expectations
that cannot be met.

She has stopped talking
because no one can make the
dark give way to light.

Skin scrapes warm concrete;
she dances to erase the
memory of him.

Bubbles hit my tongue,
and I wonder if we can
save this burning bridge.

She holds the tension
of the world inside her. Now,
watch as it burns bright.

But the thing about
loneliness is that it lives
and dies with a spark.

Come all you weary.
Lay down your weighted souls; be
sanctified in light.

These memories like
bullets cracking through my head,
and I'm going down.

And so you hold me
tight as my body shakes loose—
nine years of his name.

Our bodies tangled
on the living room floor as
you sing me to sleep.

Faith wears thin as the
black man meets sweet death to make
America great.

His blue eyes weighed down
heavy with love—your guitar
to carry you home.

Oh, we're only here
for a little while, so take
my hand and we'll fly.

And the spirit turns
to despair when you can't feel
anything small, love.

Roadside cigarette—
break to cut loose these heavy
chains holding you down.

Apologies live
in green eyes; I don't want to
fight this war tonight.

Sparks fly off her tongue
with ferocity meant to
make him feel his worth.

Unsteady, and so
you're feeding the same monsters
who left you for dead.

Two hearts set apart
by distance, and so birthday
boy has got the blues.

He leaves her painted
flowers after dark. Tears flow,
and we'll keep living.

Her bones settle with
loneliness. An empty bed
and sad songs—come home.

And fight when you feel
like flying, 'cause tomorrow
might be worth something.

We're stuck in a war.
Dead flowers and whiskey. Make
this last forever.

And what if I said
I miss the light in your eyes
when you were happy?

Lay here in the dark
with me. We'll lie to ourselves,
say this doesn't hurt.

What hurts the most? She'll
never be enough. Turn down
the lights wipe those tears.

Are you happy now?
Oh, these bones ache with fear. You
better fly, else fall.

We'll slow dance in the
middle of a coffee shop;
pretend we're alone.

So you'll disappear
again. Watch the world drift by;
you were meant for more.

You are worthy of
more than fuckboys who seek and
destroy for pleasure.

Smoke slides from your dark
lips. Get lost in the moon. Tell
me you still believe.

If I had known these
bones would carry so much pain,
still, I would love you.

Immersed in my pain
again. Don't look backwards, dear;
he will consume you.

Wear your prettiest
dress. Don't cry. Hide the scars. You'll
never be enough.

Broken guitars and
glass hearts. Don't give in. No one
likes desperation.

Child, do not tremble.
The darkest days cannot quench
the light in your eyes.

And they've already
forgotten you. Cold hands and
bright eyes—selfish girl.

Shiny screens absorb
us. Look away. She's screaming
into the abyss.

Show me how you're strong.
Don't be afraid now—we're just
drops in the ocean.

Boy, do not fret. I'm
not your home. She'll deliver
you unto the light.

I hope you find what
you're looking for. Rejoice, there's
a lesson in this.

They promise it's not
you as the door closes. Could
you love this woman?

Always wanting more—
selfish girl. Stars the same shade
as baby's big blues.

I picture you at
my door, words you'll never say
on your lips. Sweet dreams.

She trembles as he
strokes her womanhood. Mother
Earth swallows them whole.

Whiskey running through
you. Slow dance in an empty
bar. Pain dissipates.

Heavy winds crush her:
Salty tears, smoky backseat,
Yellowstone or bust.

Pluck grass from under
you. Faulty bodies deserve
love, too. You are more.

Room full of strangers.
Get lost in the music, and
say we'll be all right.

Replenish thirsty
ground. Heavy hearts believe in
love, and we shall be…

Memories seep from
her veins—to be empty and
weightless, free of him.

Oh, there's got to be
more than this. Empty eyes and
arched back. What is love?

We loiter in church
parking lots inhaling smoke
and cursing our fates.

Biography

Ashley Centers is a thirty-year-old creative. When not writing for *Home and Harvest* and *Inland 360*, she can be found reading almost anything, attempting to write something other than haiku, basking in the sun when Mother Nature allows and hiding in her cocoon when she doesn't. She enjoys live music (or all music, really), her cat, white coffee, the glorious sun, and sometimes people.

Ashley graduated from the University of Idaho with a bachelors in English with an emphasis in creative writing and a minor in journalism. She can be reached by email at **burnintruthbeloved@gmail.com**.

Made in the USA
Columbia, SC
09 August 2021